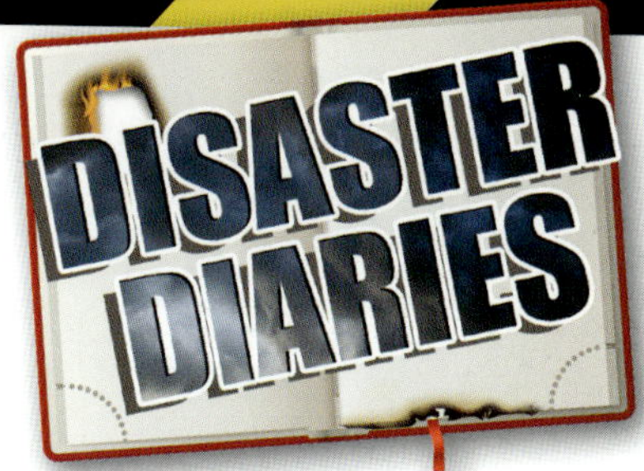

Surviving the TSUNAMI

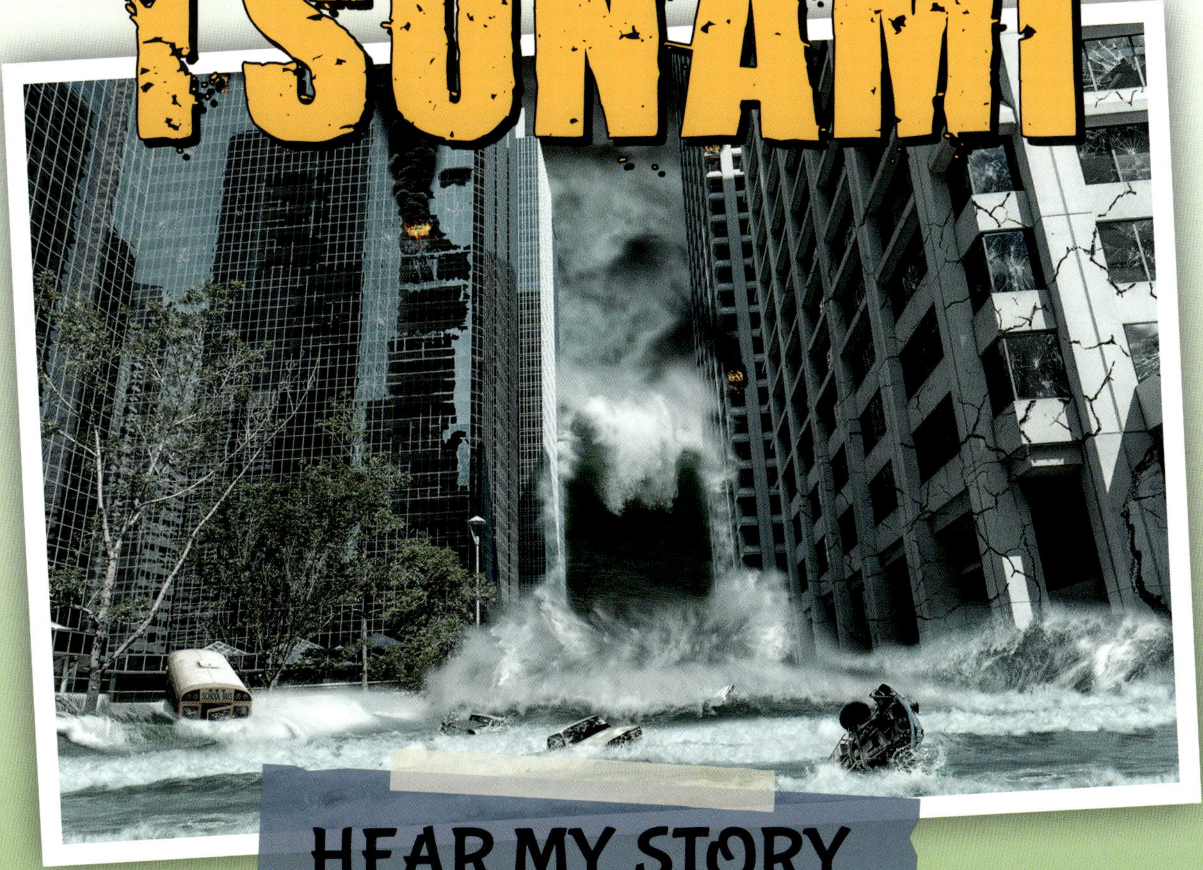

HEAR MY STORY

Sarah Eason

Author: Sarah Eason

Editorial director: Kathy Middleton

Editors: Jennifer Sanderson, and Ellen Rodger

Proofreaders: Tracey Kelly, Melissa Boyce

Editorial director: Kathy Middleton

Design: Paul Myerscough

Cover design: Margaret Amy Salter

Photo research: Rachel Blount

Production coordinator and Prepress technician: Tammy McGarr

Print coordinator: Katherine Berti

Consultant: John Farndon

Produced for Crabtree Publishing Company by Calcium

Photo Credits:
t=Top, c=Center, b=Bottom, l= Left, r=Right

Inside: Jessica Moon: p. 10; NASA: Sadatsugu Tomizawa: p. 5t; Shutterstock: Doroniuk Anastasiia: p. 14; Herwin Bahar: p. 9; BNK Maritime Photographer: p. 26; Ramunas Bruzas: p. 11; Ronnie Chua: pp. 1, 27b; Ethan Daniels: p. 19; Frans Delian: pp. 5b, 13t, 22-23, 23t, 28-29, 29r; Dushi82: pp. 15, 16-17; Kelly Headrick: p. 8; Ryan Janssens: pp. 12-13; Joko P: p. 16b; Andrew Mayovskyy: p. 20; Erpe Motret: p. 17r; SantiPhotoSS: p. 6b; Stella Sophie: p. 21; Tzido Sun: p. 4; ThamKC: p. 27t; Tjuktjuk: pp. 6-7; Tunasalmon: p. 18; Vchal: p. 25; Vismar UK: p. 24.

Cover: Wikimedia Commons: U.S. Navy photo by Photographer's Mate 3rd Class Tyler J. Clements

Publisher's Note: The story presented in this book is a fictional account based on extensive research of real-life accounts, with the aim of reflecting the true experience of victims of natural disasters.

Library and Archives Canada Cataloguing in Publication

Title: Surviving the tsunami : hear my story / Sarah Eason.
Names: Eason, Sarah, author.
Description: Series statement: Disaster diaries | Includes index.
Identifiers: Canadiana (print) 20200150170 |
Canadiana (ebook) 20200150197 |
ISBN 9780778769910 (hardcover) |
ISBN 9780778771197 (softcover) |
ISBN 9781427124487 (HTML)
Subjects: LCSH: Indian Ocean Tsunami, 2004—Juvenile literature. | LCSH: Tsunamis—Indonesia—Juvenile literature. | LCSH: Tsunamis—Juvenile literature. | LCSH: Disaster victims—Juvenile literature.
Classification: LCC GC221.5 .E27 2020 | DDC j551.46/37156—dc23

Library of Congress Cataloging-in-Publication Data

Names: Eason, Sarah, author.
Title: Surviving the tsunami : hear my story / Sarah Eason
Description: New York : Crabtree Publishing Company, [2020] |
Series: Disaster diaries |
Includes bibliographical references and index.
Identifiers: LCCN 2019053365 (print) | LCCN 2019053366 (ebook) |
ISBN 9780778769910 (hardcover) |
ISBN 9780778771197 (paperback) |
ISBN 9781427124487 (ebook)
Subjects: LCSH: Indian Ocean Tsunami, 2004--Juvenile literature. | Disaster victims--Indonesia--Juvenile literature. | Disaster relief--Indonesia--Juvenile literature.
Classification: LCC HV603 2004 .I5 E27 2020 (print) |
LCC HV603 2004 .I5 (ebook) | DDC 363.34/94092 [B]--dc23
LC record available at https://lccn.loc.gov/2019053365
LC ebook record available at https://lccn.loc.gov/2019053366

Crabtree Publishing Company
www.crabtreebooks.com 1-800-387-7650

Printed in the U.S.A./022020/CG20200102

Published in Canada
Crabtree Publishing
616 Welland Ave.
St. Catharines, Ontario
L2M 5V6

Published in the United States
Crabtree Publishing
PMB 59051
350 Fifth Avenue, 59th Floor
New York, New York 10118

Published in the United Kingdom
Crabtree Publishing
Maritime House
Basin Road North, Hove
BN41 1WR

Published in Australia
Crabtree Publishing
3 Charles Street
Coburg North
VIC, 3058

Contents

Tsunamis and Their Victims

Tsunamis are very destructive types of waves. Tsunamis destroy landscapes, wreck property, and kill or injure many people when they hit land. They are truly one of Earth's most terrifying **natural disasters**.

No Ordinary Wave

Tsunamis are not like ordinary waves. Ordinary waves happen when wind blows the surface of oceans, lakes, and other areas of water into ripples and peaks that then form waves as they gather energy. Tsunamis are not caused by wind. They are caused by natural disasters, such as undersea **earthquakes** or **volcanic eruptions**.

Deadly and Destructive

Tsunamis can cause terrible loss of life. Most people die as they are caught up in the bubbling swirl of water and then drown beneath its surface. Many people who have survived a tsunami describe the experience as like being caught up in a giant washing machine.

The largest tsunamis can be as tall as the Statue of Liberty in New York City, which is 305 feet (93 m) high. If you look at this picture, you can imagine the destruction one would cause if it hit the city.

Although drowning is the most common cause of death from a tsunami, people are also harmed by **debris** that tsunamis carry. When the monster waves hit objects such as buildings and vehicles, tsunamis smash them up and then carry parts of them along as they travel. These can include jagged metal and pieces of glass, which rip and tear flesh. They can also include larger pieces of metal and wood. If they hit a person, these can deliver a deadly blow.

This is a photograph of the tsunami that hit the coast of Japan in 2011. The water rushed inland, carrying along vehicles and other objects as it moved.

Centuries of Tsunamis

There have been many tsunamis in Earth's history. Over the course of **recorded** history, tsunamis have been known to kill tens of thousands of people.

Tsunamis smash into objects and destroy everything in their paths, including buildings, vehicles, and trees. This photograph shows the destruction caused in Banda Aceh, Indonesia, by the Indian Ocean tsunami of 2004.

ADITYA'S STORY

In this book, you can find out what it is like to live through a natural disaster by reading the fictional story of Aditya, a young boy caught up in the Indian Ocean tsunami disaster of 2004. **Look for his story on pages 6–7, 12–13, 16–17, 22–23, and 28–29.**

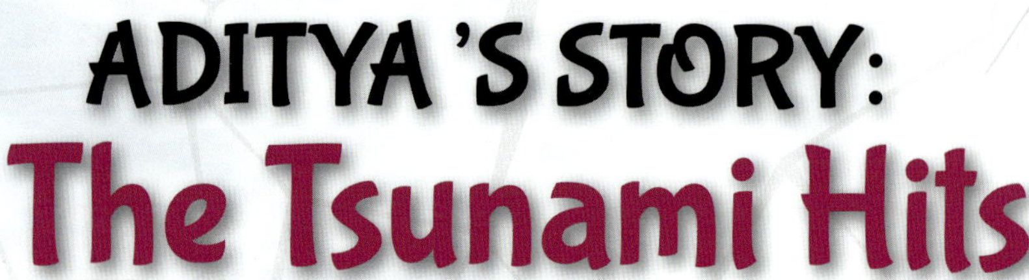

ADITYA'S STORY: The Tsunami Hits

I will never forget the morning of December 26, 2004—it was then that the tsunami hit my village and changed my life forever. That morning, I was playing freestyle soccer with my friends a little way from our village of Alue Naga, near Banda Aceh. We were all laughing and having fun. My best friend, Marthunis, and I loved practicing soccer—he was really great at dribbling. And he was showing off his skills big time that day!

I was thirsty and sweaty from playing, so I took a break and sat on a fallen tree. From there, I could see the beach and all the way out to sea, to where the men from our village fished in their boats. My dad and uncle were fishing that day. I knew they wouldn't be home until later—hopefully with a big catch.

Many people were going about their everyday lives when the tsunami hit, just like Aditya and his friends. The disaster took them completely by surprise.

DANGER

About five minutes later, everything changed. The sea suddenly looked completely different. It seemed as if the tide had gone out—all the way out. I watched closely as the sea changed again—and it changed so fast. Suddenly, a huge wave of water raced toward the shore. I couldn't believe it. I had never seen anything like it!

I will never forget the noise that the water made. It was a really loud rumbling, as if a huge train was coming near—but this was no train. I knew from everything I had learned at school that this was a deadly wave, a tsunami.

Many people were on vacation in Banda Aceh and other areas of Indonesia when the tsunami hit in 2004. Some of those who were near the ocean died when the waves surged across the beaches near their hotels.

I think about the tsunami every day, and all the people who died.

Trails of Destruction

Survivors of tsunamis describe the impact of the wave as feeling like a wall of concrete hitting them.

Tsunami waves travel at enormous speeds across an ocean. The average speed of a tsunami when it hits the shore is 30 to 40 miles per hour (48 to 64 kph). If you imagine a car traveling down a city street, it is as fast as that. Now imagine a solid wave of water moving at that speed and you can begin to see how destructive tsunamis can be.

Walls of Speeding Water

The fastest tsunamis move much more quickly than 40 miles per hour (64 kph). These superfast movers can travel at speeds ten times faster! When they hit the shore, these giant walls of water smash into anything in their paths.

Disaster after Disaster

Even after the waves have **subsided**, tsunamis continue to cause devastation. With buildings destroyed, people are left homeless. **Sanitation** becomes a problem too—without clean, running water and toilets, disease can quickly spread. Many people who live near coastlines also have businesses there, such as fishing businesses or hotels and restaurants. When these are destroyed, people lose their jobs and **incomes** as well as their homes.

VICTIMS OF THE WAVES

It is impossible to outrun a tsunami. When an earthquake took place off the coast of Chile in 1960, it caused a huge tsunami that sped toward the shore and hit just 15 minutes later. The wave rose up to 80 feet (24 m) in places and moved with such force that it carried people's homes up to 2 miles (3.2 km) inland.

The damage caused by a tsunami can cost millions of dollars to fix, and it can take years to rebuild an area after a tsunami strike.

Rebuilding After the Destruction

Rebuilding after a tsunami is very expensive, and poor countries struggle unless they receive help from wealthier **nations**. For example, when the Indian Ocean tsunami of 2004 hit, the Red Cross **charity** paid for the building of more than 2,000 new homes and gave $6 million to help people go back to work and rebuild **industries**.

The Causes of Tsunamis

Tsunamis usually take place because of other natural disasters that occur deep underwater. These can include earthquakes and volcanic eruptions.

Earthquakes and Tsunamis

Earth's crust is made up of **tectonic plates**, which shift and move against each other. As two plates push against each other, **pressure** builds up between them. The pressure can cause part of Earth's crust to buckle and move. This is an earthquake. If the sudden movement of an earthquake takes place beneath the ocean, it can **force** up a large amount of water very quickly. This is called **water displacement**. It is this water displacement that causes a tsunami to form.

Volcanoes and Tsunamis

Tsunamis can also be caused by undersea volcanic activity. For example, if a volcano collapses underwater, it can cause water displacement—and a tsunami. At other times, a volcano near the ocean may erupt, and large amounts of rock from the volcano may fall into the ocean. This, too, can cause a tsunami to form.

When two plates push against each other with a lot of force, extreme pressure is created.

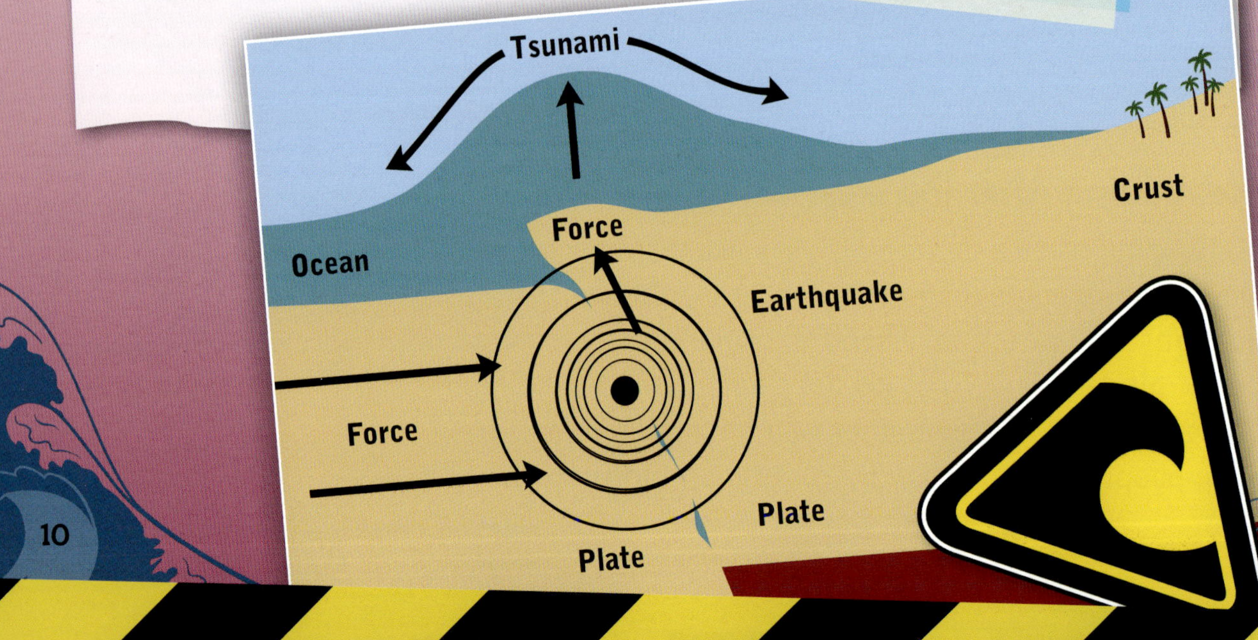

Other Causes of Tsunamis

Tsunamis can also be caused by other events. Sometimes, **landslides** and large rock falls can cause them. If a large area of land or rock falls off a cliffside and into the water below, it can cause water displacement and a tsunami.

A landslide or rock fall is particularly dangerous if it happens in an area that has high cliffs on either side of a long area of water, such as a **fjord**. The displaced water is then forced along the narrow area, pushing it into a huge wave, which can flatten anything in its path. The destruction that results can be enormous.

Glaciers are large masses of ice. They can be found in cold ocean areas. Sometimes, part of the ice breaks off and falls into the water. If a very large piece of ice breaks off, it can cause a tsunami.

VICTIMS OF THE UNDERSEA QUAKE

In 2011, the most powerful earthquake ever to hit Japan struck 42 miles (68 km) off the northeast coast. It triggered a **series** of deadly tsunamis that killed thousands of people and caused $32.6 billion in damage. Around 300,000 people lost their homes.

ADITYA 'S STORY: In the Water

When the tsunami hit, it flipped me over and over in the water. I had heard people say that being in a tsunami is like being spun around in a washing machine, but this felt way worse. I felt like I was being crushed and spun at the same time. I couldn't breathe, and I didn't know which way was up or which way was down. I kept trying to reach out and feel for the surface. But all I could feel was water. Then I felt something hard hit me on the head.

I don't know how long I was **unconscious**, but it was probably just a few seconds. All I remember was waking up and finding myself in the water, with pieces of furniture, clothes, and all kinds of things bobbing around me. I could see a plastic chair floating nearby, so I reached out for it and held on tight.

Most people have been knocked over by a wave while having fun on vacation. The force of even just a small wave can be enough to knock you off your feet. Imagine the force of being hit by a tsunami wave.

My head really ached, and I knew I had hurt it badly. My leg was hurting too—I was sure it had been cut by something. I looked up and could see a beach in the distance. I could feel the water pulling me toward it, so I just held on to the chair and hoped I'd make it to shore. I felt so weak that all I could do was just hang on and pray.

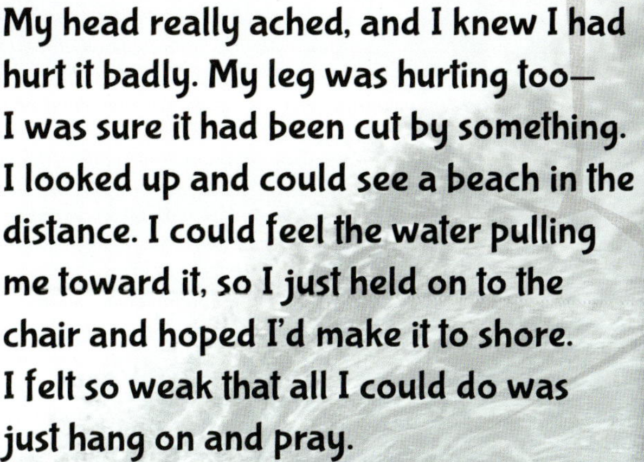

This is a photograph of Banda Aceh after the tsunami. It is littered with debris from the wave, such as furniture, parts of buildings, and belongings swept away from homes.

It seemed like forever, but finally I could feel the sand beneath my feet, and I dragged myself onto the beach. I felt my head with my hand. I could feel a big bump, and when I took my hand away, it was covered with blood. Then I looked down at my leg. It had a long cut on it, and it was trickling with blood too.

I had no idea where I was—I couldn't see anything I recognized around me. I was so hungry and thirsty too. I must have been floating in the water for hours. Then, all thoughts of food, drink, and my aching body left my mind. All along the beach were bodies.

DANGER

How Tsunamis Work

When an undersea earthquake occurs, the energy from it pushes upward, creating a bulge in the ocean surface. The energy is then forced outward along the surface of the water. The action is a little like the way a lot of ripples are created when you throw a pebble into a pond. That is why a tsunami that begins in the middle of an ocean can reach land on either side of it. For example, an undersea earthquake that takes place in the Pacific Ocean between Hawaii and California could create a tsunami that hits both areas.

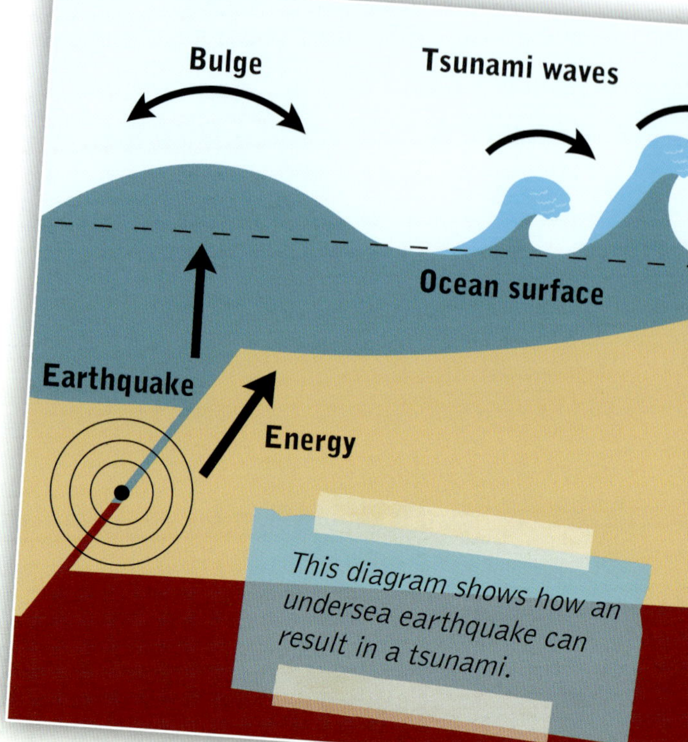

This diagram shows how an undersea earthquake can result in a tsunami.

VICTIMS OF THE WAVES

In 2004, an enormous tsunami caused by an underwater earthquake struck coastlines all around the Indian Ocean. It was one of the worst tsunamis ever recorded. It killed 230,000 people. Half of these were in Indonesia, the area closest to the earthquake center, but some of the people who died were as far away as the east coast of Africa. This was thousands of miles away from the quake center, but the waves even reached the coastline there.

Moving Quickly

The huge force from the underwater earthquake drives the tsunami forward, making it move at incredible speeds. A tsunami can travel at hundreds of miles per hour in deep water. At this point, the tsunami may not be very tall at all. This changes as it approaches shallower water near the coastline.

Getting Bigger

Near the coastline, the energy of the tsunami is compressed, or squashed together, by the shallow water and the land. Now, instead of moving the wave forward at great speed, the energy forces the water upward. The tsunami slows down but grows much taller. Its height can increase quickly as it moves toward the shore. The tsunami now travels at speeds of typically 30 miles per hour (48 kph). It usually arrives at the shore in a series of waves.

The 2004 Indian Ocean tsunami was so powerful that it ripped trees from the ground and carried along huge ships, dumping them far inland. These tree roots were ripped from the ground by the tsunami.

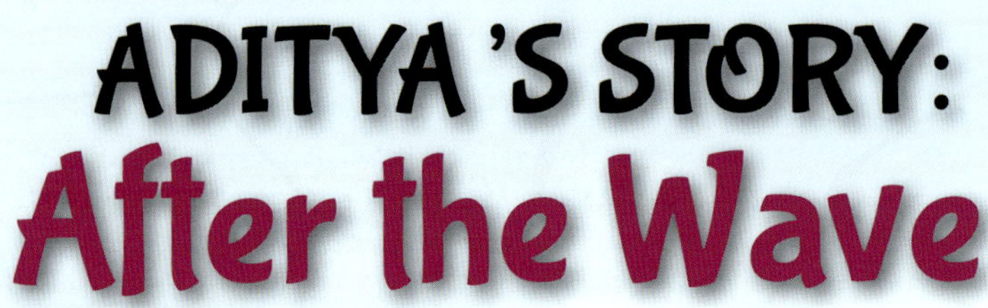

ADITYA'S STORY: After the Wave

It was horrible to see all the bodies on the beach. I will never forget it. Even now, I still have nightmares when I remember what I saw that day. At the time, although I was shocked, somehow my brain just turned off. I guess a **survival instinct** kicked in. I could see some bottles of water floating near the roots of a **mangrove**, so I waded over and picked them up. I drank one quickly, then another. Then I put the rest of the bottles on a mattress that had washed up near the mangrove. After that, I collapsed on the mattress and slept for hours.

When I woke up, it was getting dark. I felt really scared—was anyone looking for me, and when would they come? My mom had been visiting my grandma at Fakinah Hospital near Banda Aceh that day. There, she would have been safe from the tsunami but would be desperate to know what had happened to me. I was sure she would be looking for me. And I was so worried about my dad. Had he managed to survive the wave, way out at sea on his boat? I prayed he was safe.

DANGER

Huge amounts of debris from the tsunami were washed up around the roots of mangroves along the Indonesian coastline.

My leg was hurting too much to try and walk to find help, so I lay down again on the mattress and looked up at the stars. I couldn't stop thinking about the wave and what had happened—it seemed like a story from a disaster movie. Yet, somehow, it was real.

When morning came, I sat up and looked around me. More things had washed up onto the beach, and the bodies were still there. Then I heard a shout! I looked over to where the noise came from and could see two men. I yelled, "Help! Help!" and waved my hands in the air. The men ran toward me. They lifted me up and told me that everything would be OK. Then one of the men carried me to the road, while the other one walked alongside us, talking to someone on his cell phone. The men helped me into their truck and drove me to Fakinah Hospital.

These people are lighting candles to remember the many people who died during the 2004 tsunami in Banda Aceh.

Even huge mangroves, like this one, were ripped from the ground by the 2004 tsunami.

Where Tsunamis Happen

Most tsunamis take place in the Pacific Ocean—in fact, 80 percent of all tsunamis happen there. This is because the ocean lies over the enormous Pacific plate, which rubs up or dips under a number of **continental** plates. Pressure from the plate movement in the Pacific Ocean can create undersea earthquakes—and tsunamis.

A Ring of Fire

Also in the Pacific area is the Ring of Fire, which is a region of enormous volcanic activity. Many of the tsunamis that take place in the Pacific Ocean are caused by volcanic activity.

The Ring of Fire lies near many countries that may be hit by tsunamis, including Japan and Indonesia.

Beyond the Pacific

Although most tsunamis take place in the Pacific Ocean, they can occur elsewhere too. For example, we know that tsunamis can take place in fjords, which are long areas of inland water surrounded by high cliffs. Tsunamis can also happen in cold, northern regions such as Alaska, which have glaciers. When large sheets of ice fall into surrounding water, the water displacement can result in a tsunami.

We also know that tsunamis have taken place in other oceans in Earth's history. For example, a **megatsunami** occurred in the North Sea 7,000 years ago. As it hit the shoreline and islands of northern Britain, it wiped out many coastal villages.

These bubbles are rising from an undersea volcano near the Lesser Sunda Islands in Indonesia, which is near the Ring of Fire.

VICTIMS OF THE GIANT WAVE

In Alaska in 1958, an earthquake caused a giant rockfall and broke off part of a glacier at one end of Lituya Bay. This caused a megatsunami that rose to an incredible 1,500 feet (457 m) when it struck land at the far side of the bay. Bill and Vivian Swanson were asleep on their boat in the bay when the tsunami hit. It carried their boat along on top of the wave like a surfboard. The boat was broken to pieces, but amazingly, the couple survived and floated in the bay on a dinghy until they were rescued.

Danger Zones

Norway, in Europe, has many fjords and has experienced tsunamis in the past. Since 1888, 10 tsunamis have happened there, killing 144 people.

Different areas of the world are known to be at particular risk from tsunamis. Many of these are around the dangerous Ring of Fire, but these are not the only danger spots on the globe. Far away from the Pacific, places that have fjords, such as Alaska and Norway, are on the high-risk list.

In the Path of Disaster

The Ring of Fire runs from the bottom of Chile in South America, north to Alaska in North America. It passes through Japan and the Philippines and continues south to New Zealand. Any of the places along this path are in the tsunami risk zone.

A Spreading Ring of Danger

The danger from the Ring of Fire also affects places beyond the Pacific Ocean. The Pacific is connected to other ocean areas. If an undersea disaster happens in an area of the Pacific near another ocean, it can cause a tsunami to happen in that ocean. For example, an earthquake in the Ring of Fire region caused the devastating tsunami of 2004 in the Indian Ocean.

Shaping Disaster

The shape of the coastal land in some tsunami danger zones also has a big effect on how damaging the waves are when they hit. If the coastline is flat, the waves have little to **resist** them, and they push far inland. The destruction in these places is much greater than it would be if the tsunamis hit more hilly coastlines. Tsunami danger zones with particularly low-lying coasts include the Maldive Islands and low-lying coastal areas of Indonesia.

Tsunamis in North America

All coastal areas in the United States and Canada are also at risk from tsunamis, but places along the Pacific coast are most in danger.

VICTIMS OF THE ISLAND

In December 1992, an earthquake took place near a small island in Indonesia named Babi Island. When the tsunami hit the flat and low-lying coastal areas on the shores of the island, it had risen to 23 feet (7 m) above sea level. The wave washed away every single wooden home on the island and killed 252 people. Just a few managed to survive to tell the tale.

The Maldive Islands are very flat and have many low-lying communities and resorts. A tsunami there would be devastating.

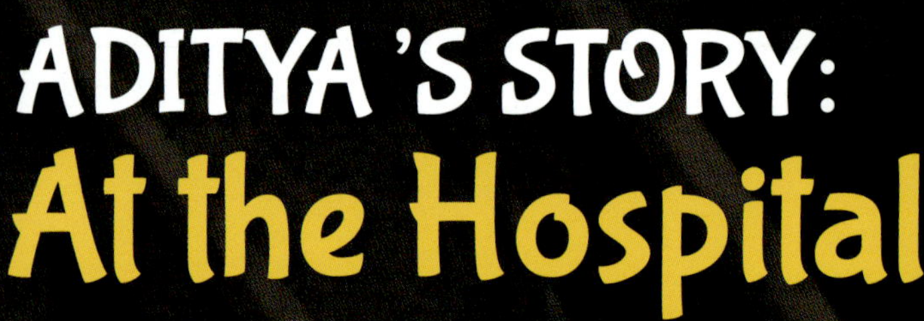

ADITYA 'S STORY: At the Hospital

At the hospital, there were people everywhere. Some had cuts and bruises. Others had worse injuries—broken arms and legs, head injuries, and legs and feet that had been shredded by broken glass and other sharp objects carried by the wave. Many people were dead—lying on the floor throughout the hospital, covered with sheets.

I closed my eyes, wanting to keep everything out. A doctor asked me who I was and where I came from as he treated my head and leg. I told him I was Aditya and that I came from Alue Naga. I said that my grandma was here at the hospital. A nurse told the doctor that she thought she knew who my grandma was. The nurse said that she had been talking to my mom earlier that morning. She said my mom was desperate to find me.

Many young children lost their parents or had parents who were very badly hurt during the 2004 tsunami. This little girl had to care for her baby sibling after the disaster.

The nurse left the room to try and find my mom. Ten minutes later, my mom came running through the door. She threw her arms around me and held me so close that I could hardly breathe. She was crying and crying, and telling me over and over that she loved me. She said she had been so scared that she might have lost me. I couldn't stop crying too.

I asked my mom if my dad was at the hospital too. She got really quiet. She took a deep breath and held me close again. Then she looked at me and told me softly that my dad hadn't come back from sea. She said that she hadn't given up hope, but we had to prepare ourselves for the possibility that he had been lost, caught up in the tsunami wave. We both cried again—we had found each other, but the thought of losing my dad hurt so much that I didn't think I could stand it.

Aid workers helped survivors after the 2004 tsunami. They gave out food, water, and information. People were also treated in **temporary** *medical tents when hospitals could not cope with the number of people needing help.*

How Science Can Fight Tsunamis

Tsunamis have brought about such terrible destruction in our recent history that scientists are more determined than ever to understand these natural disasters. Scientists cannot keep tsunamis from happening—they are natural forces of nature that we have no control over. However, the more scientists understand about tsunamis and their causes, the more they can do to help save lives.

Looking at the Land

After a tsunami, scientists visit the area of land it hit to study what happened there. They take **samples** of the **sediment** and debris washed inland by the tsunami. They study the number of layers in the sediment and how thick they are so that they can learn about the wave. If there are many layers in the samples, it tells scientists that a series of tsunami waves hit. If the layers are very thick, it means that the force with which the tsunami moved was very powerful.

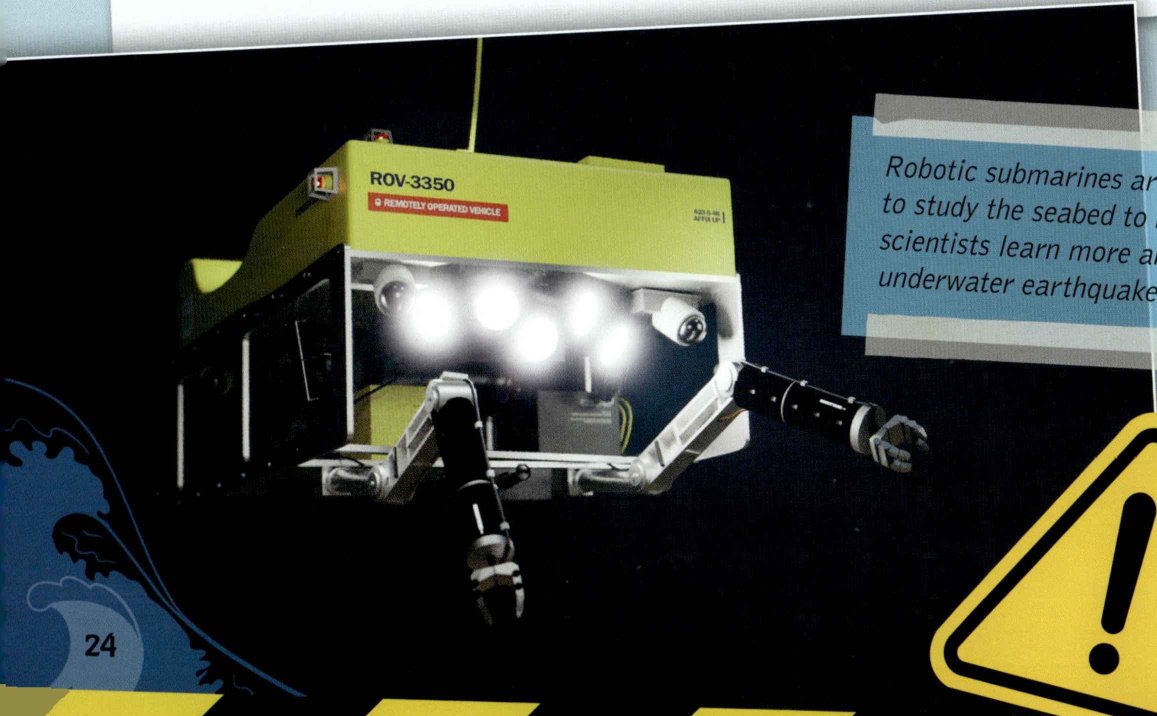

Robotic submarines are used to study the seabed to help scientists learn more about underwater earthquakes.

Looking under the Sea

Scientists also study the seafloor to find out more about tsunamis. They drill into the seafloor to take samples in areas where undersea earthquakes have caused tsunamis. The samples can show details about the tectonic plates in the area and the seabed above them, and they explain why earthquakes occurred there.

*Scientists use **seismographs** to carefully monitor undersea plates to try to **predict** when an earthquake might occur next.*

Looking from Space

Scientists also look at **satellite images** taken from space of the area before and after a tsunami hit. These images can show how far the tsunami moved inland, how wide an area it covered, and how much it affected farmland, buildings, and the natural environment.

VICTIMS OF THE SEAWATER

Scientists talk to the victims of tsunamis to learn more about the behavior of these killer waves. In a study of more than 4,500 injured people in Sri Lanka after the 2004 tsunami in the Indian Ocean, scientists discovered that 28 percent of them had lung problems caused by almost drowning. The problems are caused when seawater washes **bacteria** and **silt** into the lungs, where they become trapped. This leads to infections that make it difficult for people to breathe.

Protecting People

To help protect people against future tsunamis, scientists and organizations around the world have worked together to set up a **network** of **buoys** in areas that are at risk of tsunamis. The buoys are all **connected** to **sensors** on the seabed.

This tsunami detection buoy is near the Nicobar Islands off the coast of India. It checks activity on the seabed there.

Sensing Danger

The sensors measure changes in water pressure at certain points above the seabed. If a tsunami passes over the sensors, they will detect it. The buoys connected to the sensors then send messages to satellites in space, telling them about the changes in water pressure.

Sending Warnings

The satellites send the information from the sensors to tsunami warning centers around the world. Early warning systems are then **activated** to alert people in high-risk areas that a tsunami might be about to take place. This gives people valuable time in which to leave dangerous, low-lying areas and get to higher ground where they are in less danger from a tsunami wave.

Making Plans

People who live in tsunami danger zones are also taught how to protect themselves if a tsunami does occur. In places like Hawaii, **residents** are given a tsunami evacuation map that shows safe places on the island to go to in the event of a tsunami. In Japan, people are educated about tsunami dangers and survival techniques. Schools even teach their students about the dangers of these killer waves and what to do if one hits.

*Japan has built many **seawalls** to try to lessen the impact of tsunami waves.*

Emergency Kit

People near coastlines under threat from tsunamis are also told to keep an emergency kit ready in case they have to **evacuate** the area quickly. This usually contains things such as a radio, battery-powered flashlight, drinking water, and a first aid kit.

PROTECTING POTENTIAL VICTIMS

Japan has put deep-sea **tsunami detectors** and early warning systems in place so that its scientists can carefully watch all activity off the country's coasts and warn people well ahead of a tsunami hit.

Scientists estimate that by the year 2025, the number of people living near coastlines will have grown by 23 percent. Scientists are concerned that super tsunamis of the future could have catastrophic consequences if they hit large towns or cities along the coasts, as shown by this artist's illustration of an imaginary tsunami.

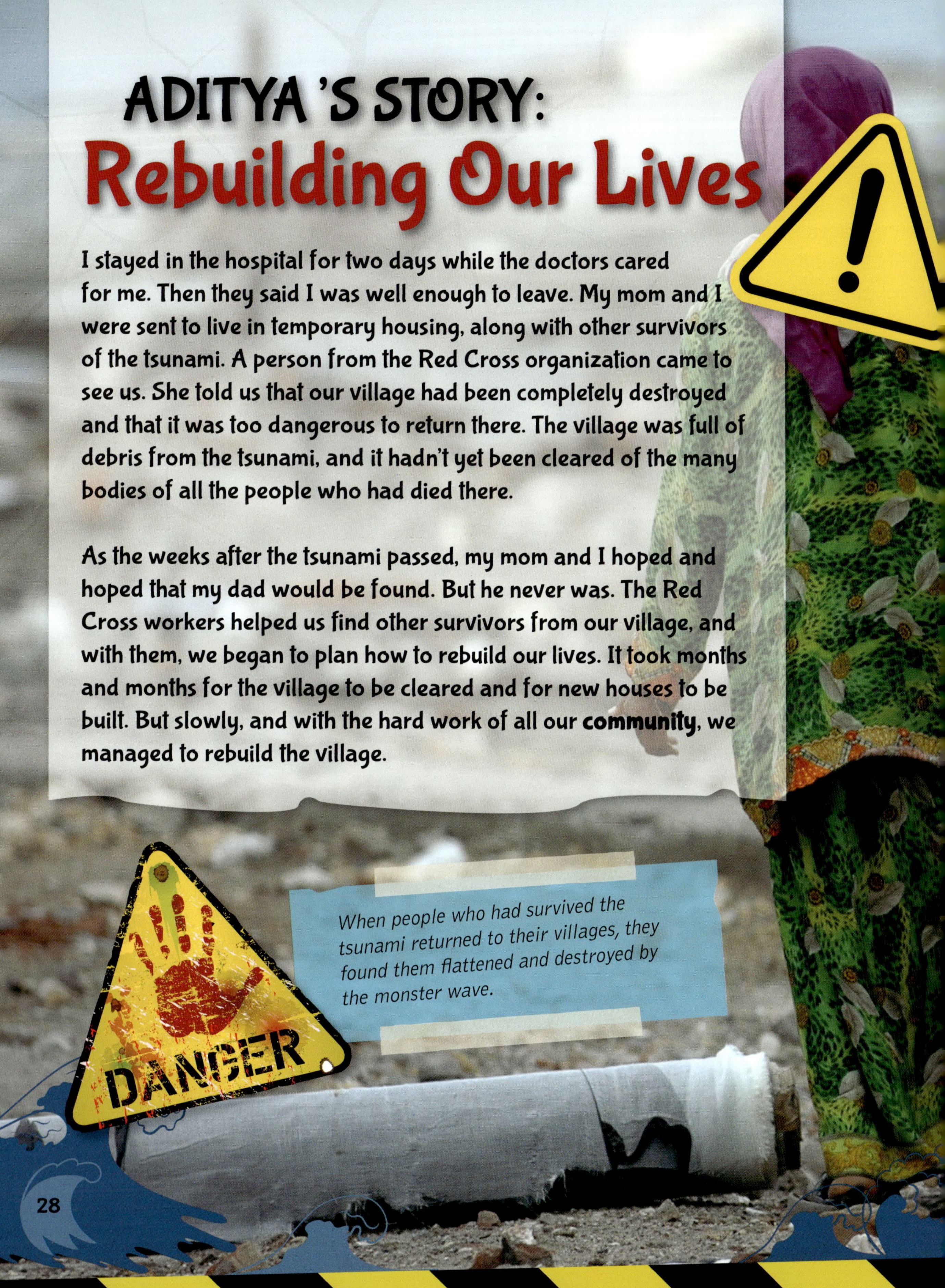

ADITYA 'S STORY:
Rebuilding Our Lives

I stayed in the hospital for two days while the doctors cared for me. Then they said I was well enough to leave. My mom and I were sent to live in temporary housing, along with other survivors of the tsunami. A person from the Red Cross organization came to see us. She told us that our village had been completely destroyed and that it was too dangerous to return there. The village was full of debris from the tsunami, and it hadn't yet been cleared of the many bodies of all the people who had died there.

As the weeks after the tsunami passed, my mom and I hoped and hoped that my dad would be found. But he never was. The Red Cross workers helped us find other survivors from our village, and with them, we began to plan how to rebuild our lives. It took months and months for the village to be cleared and for new houses to be built. But slowly, and with the hard work of all our **community**, we managed to rebuild the village.

When people who had survived the tsunami returned to their villages, they found them flattened and destroyed by the monster wave.

When my mom and I finally moved into our new home, we felt a sense of peace at having returned home. But we were also so sad. We had lost so much—not only my dad, but also many family members and friends. My uncle had been lost with my dad, and my aunt and all my cousins had died in the tsunami. Marthunis and my other friends had all been killed too—rescue workers had found their bodies in the search for survivors. There was so much loss that it was hard to bear.

My mom doesn't like me to be far from her now—she is always anxious and wants to keep me close to her so she knows I am safe. I'm not the same boy I was before the disaster—I don't think I ever will be. But together, my mom, my grandma, and I are trying to start over. We survived the tsunami, and now we have begun our lives again.

Many people had to live in tents for months after the tsunami disaster of 2004.

Glossary

activated Turned on or made to work

bacteria Tiny organisms that can cause illness and disease

buoys Floating objects that are anchored in water to warn of danger

charity An organization that tries to help people in need

community A group of people who live in one place, such as a village or a town

connected Joined to

continental On or part of a continent, which is one of the seven large masses, or areas, of land on Earth

debris Waste or bits of material left over from an event such as a disaster

earthquakes Violent shakings of the ground caused by movements beneath Earth's surface

evacuate To clear an area of people because it is dangerous

fictional Made up, not true

fjord A long body of water surrounded on both sides by tall cliffs

force To move something by physical strength

incomes Money that people earn

industries Types of work such as mining, building, or making food

landslides The sliding of loose earth and rock down a steep slope

mangrove A type of tree that grows in hot countries near areas of water, such as the ocean

megatsunami A giant tsunami

nation People who belong to one country

natural disasters Disasters caused by nature, not human-made

network A system of connections

predict To say when something will happen

pressure The force acting on a surface

recorded Written or noted down

residents The people who live somewhere

resist To go against or to fight against

samples Sections of something taken by a scientist to find out more about it

sanitation Cleanliness

satellite images Photographs taken from space by satellites

seawalls Walls that are built along the coastline to try to keep out tsunamis and other large waves

sediment Material that settles at the bottom of water

seismographs Instruments that measure movement beneath Earth's crust

sensors Tools that can sense things such as movement or heat in the surrounding area

series More than one

silt Very fine mud that settles at the bottom of water

subsided Moved down to a lower level

survival instinct An urge to survive, or live

tectonic plates The pieces of Earth's crust that fit together

temporary Not permanent

tsunami detectors Machines that sense the movement of tsunamis

unconscious Asleep, not awake

volcanic eruptions Explosions of hot liquid rock from volcanoes

water displacement The movement of water

Learning More

Learn more about tsunamis and their dangers.

Books

Bailer, Darice. *Indian Ocean Tsunami Survival Stories.* Momentum, 2016.

Brundle, Joanna. *Tsunamis and Floods*. Kidhaven, 2019.

Larson, Kirsten. *Tsunamis*. Rourke Educational Media, 2015.

Rose, Simon. *Tsunami Readiness*. Crabtree Publishing, 2019.

Websites

Take a look at this video about tsunamis at:
https://easyscienceforkids.com/best-tsunami-facts-video-for-kids

Discover more about the science of tsunamis at:
https://www.natgeokids.com/au/discover/geography/physical-geography/tsunamis/

Read more about the power of tsunamis at:
www.ducksters.com/science/earth_science/tsunamis.php

Learn how people prepare for a tsunami disaster at:
www.ready.gov/tsunamis

Index

About the Author

Sarah Eason has written many children's books, including books about science, geography, art, and history. She enjoys researching subjects such as natural disasters and finding out about the science behind these phenomenal events.